THE HEART
TOPICAL
BIBLE

Christian T. Howell Sr

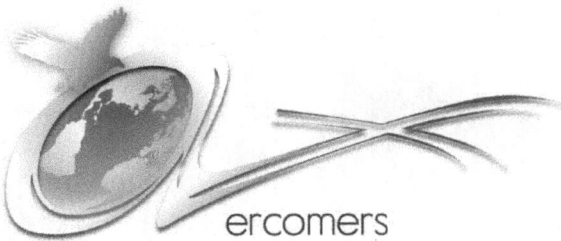

ercomers

ISBN: 978-1-7337342-1-9 (Paperback)

First printing, 2019

Christian Howell Sr.
P.O. Box 3603
Phenix City, AL, 36869

www.overcomersmovement.org

The heart…one of the smallest organs in the body, has one of the greatest responsibilities for the entire body. Your heart is vital to your health and nearly everything that goes on in your body. Without the heart's pumping action, blood can't move throughout your body. Let me briefly explain, your blood carries the oxygen and nutrients that your organs need to work well. Also, your blood carries carbon dioxide (internal waste) to your lungs so you can exhale it. The heart is at the center of your circulatory system, which is a network of blood vessels that delivers blood to every part of your body. Blood carries oxygen and other important nutrients that all body organs need to stay healthy and to work properly. In plain terms, the heart is responsible for circulating blood throughout your body that keeps it warm and alive.

If you were to look in a dictionary, the heart would be defined as a hollow muscular organ that by its rhythmic contraction acts as a force or a pump maintaining the circulation of the blood, the emotional or moral nature of a person, or one's innermost character or feelings. It would also be defined as "the center" of a thing. If you were to do a medical study on it, you would learn that it is about the size of a fist, weighs less than a pound, has four chambers, and many other fascinating facts. Even after centuries of studying it, it is still one of the most dynamic and intriguing components of the body that leave its students and scholars in awe!

While we are exploring the subject of the heart, it is important to realize that everything that exists has a heart. Every person, every group, every city, every nation, every church, and every system all have a heart. There's a pulse and rhythm that dictates the health, speed, and stability of everything that you encounter and live in. While agreeing that everything that exists has a heart, scripture will confirm that even God has a heart (Genesis 6:6 & Jeremiah 3:15). He has emotions and a center of being, which is defined as Love.

Another important truth that we can grasp from that reality is that oftentimes, God influences the affairs of the earth and man my moving of the heart of mankind. It is not always necessary for Him to personally involve Himself or send angels to accomplish His agenda. His power and wisdom creates influence in the hearts of humanity. For example, when He was ready for His children to leave Egypt, the Bible says that God hardened Pharaoh's heart (Exodus 4:21). Proverbs 21:1 also explicitly declares it! Yes angels were released to execute His plan, but it was ultimately His moving on the heart of the king that caused the release.

The heart is truly amazing. When our actions appear sincere, genuine, and pure, our heart will betray us and show the truth to God. Jeremiah said that the heart is deceitful; there's a chance that it will fool and mislead you (Numbers 15:39 & Jeremiah 17:9). It may seem insignificant, but the status of our heart determines whether the offering that we give is acceptable or not (Exodus 35:5 & 2 Corinthians 9:7).

As you meditate on different scriptures about your heart, I want you to be reminded that to really engage God, you must do it with all of your heart (Luke 10:27).

Life is going to happen. People will be people. Your adversary will constantly and consistently do anything to discourage and damage your heart so that you don't go forward in life (Numbers 32:7,9). He will sow seeds that are aimed at your heart to cause you to miss your target!

It is important that you protect your heart (Proverbs 4:23). Keep your heart soft, pliable, and watered with the life-giving Word of God (Ezekiel 36:26-27). Don't allow yourself to become entangled and consumed with the cares of life and the rewards that this world can offer (Matthew 6:21). And at the end of the day, God will strengthen and sustain your heart, if you give it to Him and allow Him to lead you (Psalms 73:26).

I pray that God's peace, which is able to guard and keep our hearts from trouble and distress, will examine your heart, mend your heart, satisfy your heart, and then give to you the desires of your heart. I pray that you will allow Him to instruct you on how to keep your heart pure so that you can ascend your assigned mountain.

***This is not an inclusive list of scriptures concerting the heart.

Confessions Over My Heart

I give the Word first place in my life. I make my schedule around Your Word! Your Word is Truth and forever settled in Heaven; therefore, I establish Your Word upon this Earth. Your Word is a lamp to my feet and a light to my path. It is quick and powerful and sharper than a two-edged sword. I have hidden Your Word in my heart that I might not sin against You. I plant the Incorruptible Seed of Your Word in my heart. It is abiding in my spirit, growing in me mightily, and producing Your nature in my life.

My heart is pure, and remains pure.

As a man thinks in his heart, so is he; therefore, all of my thoughts are positive. I do not allow Satan to use my spirit as a garbage dump by meditating on negative things that he offers me.

Because I meditate on Your Word, You keep my heart healthy and peaceful.

I receive the desires of my heart because my heart is fixed on You.

I trust You more than I trust myself. Therefore, my heart is free from confusion, cares, and fatigue.

I am kind and tenderhearted to others. I forgive them as God in Christ has forgiven me.

I believe in my heart, and confess with my mouth that I am saved and redeemed from poverty, sickness, destruction, disease, and death.

I have a willing and generous heart; therefore, You supply all of my needs. I live in abundance and overflow.

My heart is free from deceit and deception. I clearly hear my Father's voice and we have free fellowship together.

I have an understanding heart. My discernment and judgment are accurate and unbiased.

I have and operate in singleness of heart. My affections are not manipulated.

I trust in the Lord with all my heart, and I lean not to my own understanding.

OLD
TESTAMENT

GENESIS

Genesis 6:6 And it repented the LORD that he had made man on the earth, and it grieved him at his heart.

Genesis 8:21 And the LORD smelled a sweet savour; and the LORD said in his heart, I will not again curse the ground any more for man's sake; for the imagination of man's heart is evil from his youth; neither will I again smite any more every thing living, as I have done..

Genesis 20:5 Said he not unto me, She is my sister? and she, even she herself said, He is my brother: in the integrity of my heart and innocency of my hands have I done this.

Genesis 20:6 And God said unto him in a dream, Yea, I know that thou didst this in the integrity of thy heart; for I also withheld thee from sinning against me: therefore suffered I thee not to touch her.

Genesis 27:41 And Esau hated Jacob because of the blessing wherewith his father blessed him: and Esau said in his heart, The days of mourning for my father are at hand; then will I slay my brother Jacob.

Genesis 45:26 And told him, saying, Joseph is yet alive, and he is governor over all the land of Egypt. And Jacob's heart fainted, for he believed them not.

EXODUS

Exodus 4:21 And the LORD said unto Moses, When thou goest to return into Egypt, see that thou do all those wonders before Pharaoh, which I have put in thine hand: but I will harden his heart, that he shall not let the people go.

Exodus 7:3 And I will harden Pharaoh's heart, and multiply my signs and my wonders in the land of Egypt.

Exodus 7:13 And he hardened Pharaoh's heart, that he hearkened not unto them; as the LORD had said. Exodus 7:14 And the LORD said unto Moses, Pharaoh's heart is hardened, he refuseth to let the people go.

Exodus 8:19 Then the magicians said unto Pharaoh, This is the finger of God: and Pharaoh's heart was hardened, and he hearkened not unto them; as the LORD had said.

Exodus 9:14 For I will at this time send all my plagues upon thine heart, and upon thy servants, and upon thy people; that thou mayest know that there is none like me in all the earth.

Exodus 10:1 And the LORD said unto Moses, Go in unto Pharaoh: for I have hardened his heart, and the heart of his servants, that I might shew these my signs before him:

Exodus 23:9 Also thou shalt not oppress a stranger: for ye know the heart of a stranger, seeing ye were strangers in the land of Egypt.

Exodus 25:2 Speak unto the children of Israel, that they bring me an offering: of every man that giveth it willingly with his heart ye shall take my offering.

Exodus 35:5 Take ye from among you an offering unto the LORD: whosoever is of a willing heart, let him bring it, an offering of the LORD; gold, and silver, and brass,

Exodus 35:21 And they came, every one whose heart stirred him up, and every one whom his spirit made willing, and they brought the LORD'S offering to the work of the tabernacle of the congregation, and for all his service, and for the holy garments.

Exodus 35:26 And all the women whose heart stirred them up in wisdom spun goats' hair.

Exodus 35:29 The children of Israel brought a willing offering unto the LORD, every man and woman, whose heart made them willing to bring for all manner of work, which the LORD had commanded to be made by the hand of Moses.

Exodus 36:2 And Moses called Bezaleel and Aholiab, and every wise hearted man, in whose heart the LORD had put wisdom, even every one whose heart stirred him up to come unto the work to do it:

LEVITICUS

Leviticus 19:17 Thou shalt not hate thy brother in thine heart: thou shalt in any wise rebuke thy neighbour, and not suffer sin upon him.

NUMBERS

Numbers 15:39 And it shall be unto you for a fringe, that ye may look upon it, and remember all the commandments of the LORD, and do them; and that ye seek not after your own heart and your own eyes, after which ye use to go a whoring:

Numbers 32:7 And wherefore discourage ye the heart of the children of Israel from going over into the land which the LORD hath given them?

Numbers 32:9 For when they went up unto the valley of Eshcol, and saw the land, they discouraged the heart of the children of Israel, that they should not go into the land which the LORD had given them.

DEUTERONOMY

Deuteronomy 1:28 Whither shall we go up? our brethren have discouraged our heart, saying, The people is greater and taller than we; the cities are great and walled up to heaven; and moreover we have seen the sons of the Anakims there.

Deuteronomy 2:30 But Sihon king of Heshbon would not let us pass by him: for the LORD thy God hardened his spirit, and made his heart obstinate, that he might deliver him into thy hand, as appeareth this day.

Deuteronomy 4:29 But if from thence thou shalt seek the LORD thy God, thou shalt find him, if thou seek him with all thy heart and with all thy soul.

Deuteronomy 5:29 O that there were such an heart in them, that they would fear me, and keep all my commandments always, that it might be well with them, and with their children for ever!

Deuteronomy 6:5 And thou shalt love the LORD thy God with all thine heart, and with all thy soul, and with all thy might.

Deuteronomy 7:17 If thou shalt say in thine heart, These nations are more than I; how can I dispossess them?

Deuteronomy 8:2 And thou shalt remember all the way which the LORD thy God led thee these forty years in the wilderness, to humble thee, and to prove thee, to know what was in thine heart, whether thou wouldest keep his commandments, or no.

Deuteronomy 8:14 Then thine heart be lifted up, and thou forget the LORD thy God, which brought thee forth out of the land of Egypt, from the house of bondage;

Deuteronomy 8:17 And thou say in thine heart, My power and the might of mine hand hath gotten me this wealth.

Deuteronomy 9:4 Speak not thou in thine heart, after that the LORD thy God hath cast them out from before thee, saying, For my righteousness the LORD hath brought me in to possess this land: but for the wickedness of these nations the LORD doth drive them out from before thee.

Deuteronomy 9:5 Not for thy righteousness, or for the uprightness of thine heart, dost thou go to possess their land: but for the wickedness of these nations the LORD thy God doth drive them out from before thee, and that he may perform the word which the LORD sware unto thy fathers, Abraham, Isaac, and Jacob.

Deuteronomy 10:12 And now, Israel, what doth the LORD thy God require of thee, but to fear the LORD thy God, to walk in all his ways, and to love him, and to serve the LORD thy God with all thy heart and with all thy soul,

Deuteronomy 10:16 Circumcise therefore the foreskin of your heart, and be no more stiffnecked.

Deuteronomy 11:16 Take heed to yourselves, that your heart be not deceived, and ye turn aside, and serve other gods, and worship them;

Deuteronomy 15:7 If there be among you a poor man of one of thy brethren within any of thy gates in thy land which the LORD thy God giveth thee, thou shalt not harden thine heart, nor shut thine hand from thy poor brother:

Deuteronomy 15:9 Beware that there be not a thought in thy wicked heart, saying, The seventh year, the year of release, is at hand; and thine eye be evil against thy poor brother, and thou givest him nought; and he cry unto the LORD against thee, and it be sin unto thee.

Deuteronomy 15:10 Thou shalt surely give him, and thine heart shall not be grieved when thou givest unto him: because that for this thing the LORD thy God shall bless thee in all thy works, and in all that thou puttest thine hand unto.

Deuteronomy 20:8 And the officers shall speak further unto the people, and they shall say, What man is there that is fearful and fainthearted? let him go and return unto his house, lest his brethren's heart faint as well as his heart.

Deuteronomy 28:65 And among these nations shalt thou find no ease, neither shall the sole of thy foot have rest: but the LORD shall give thee there a trembling heart, and failing of eyes, and sorrow of mind:

Deuteronomy 28:67 In the morning thou shalt say, Would God it were even! and at even thou shalt say, Would God it were morning! for the fear of thine heart wherewith thou shalt fear, and for the sight of thine eyes which thou shalt see.

Deuteronomy 29:18 Lest there should be among you man, or woman, or family, or tribe, whose heart turneth away this day from the LORD our God, to go and serve the gods of these nations; lest there should be among you a root that beareth gall and wormwood;

Deuteronomy 29:19 And it come to pass, when he heareth the words of this curse, that he bless himself in his heart, saying, I shall have peace, though I walk in the imagination of mine heart, to add drunkenness to thirst:

Deuteronomy 30:6 And the LORD thy God will circumcise thine heart, and the heart of thy seed, to love the LORD thy God with all thine heart, and with all thy soul, that thou mayest live.

Deuteronomy 30:14 But the word is very nigh unto thee, in thy mouth, and in thy heart, that thou mayest do it.

JOSHUA

Joshua 5:1 And it came to pass, when all the kings of the Amorites, which were on the side of Jordan westward, and all the kings of the Canaanites, which were by the sea, heard that the LORD had dried up the waters of Jordan from before the children of Israel, until we were passed over, that their heart melted, neither was there spirit in them any more, because of the children of Israel.

Joshua 24:23 Now therefore put away, said he, the strange gods which are among you, and incline your heart unto the LORD God of Israel.

Judges 16:17 That he told her all his heart, and said unto her, There hath not come a razor upon mine head; for I have been a Nazarite unto God from my mother's womb: if I be shaven, then my strength will go from me, and I shall become weak, and be like any other man.

1 Samuel

1Samuel 1:13 Now Hannah, she spake in her heart; only her lips moved, but her voice was not heard: therefore Eli thought she had been drunken.

1Samuel 4:13 And when he came, lo, Eli sat upon a seat by the wayside watching: for his heart trembled for the ark of God. And when the man came into the city, and told it, all the city cried out.

1Samuel 10:9 And it was so, that when he had turned his back to go from Samuel, God gave him another heart: and all those signs came to pass that day.

1

Samuel 13:14 But now thy kingdom shall not continue: the LORD hath sought him a man after his own heart, and the LORD hath commanded him to be captain over his people, because thou hast not kept that which the LORD commanded thee.

1Samuel 16:7 But the LORD said unto Samuel, Look not on his countenance, or on the height of his stature; because I have refused him: for the LORD seeth not as man seeth; for man looketh on the outward appearance, but the LORD looketh on the heart.

1Samuel 17:32 And David said to Saul, Let no man's heart fail because of him; thy servant will go and fight with this Philistine.

1Samuel 21:12 And David laid up these words in his heart, and was sore afraid of Achish the king of Gath.

1Samuel 24:5 And it came to pass afterward, that David's heart smote him, because he had cut off Saul's skirt.

1Samuel 25:37 But it came to pass in the morning, when the wine was gone out of Nabal, and his wife had told him these things, that his heart died within him, and he became as a stone.

2 Samuel

2Samuel 6:16 And as the ark of the LORD came into the city of David, Michal Saul's daughter looked through a window, and saw king David leaping and dancing before the LORD; and she despised him in her heart.

2Samuel 17:10 And he also that is valiant, whose heart is as the heart of a lion, shall utterly melt: for all Israel knoweth that thy father is a mighty man, and they which be with him are valiant men.

2Samuel 19:14 And he bowed the heart of all the men of Judah, even as the heart of one man; so that they sent this word unto the king, Return thou, and all thy servants.

2Samuel 24:10 And David's heart smote him after that he had numbered the people. And David said unto the LORD, I have sinned greatly in that I have done: and now, I beseech thee, O LORD, take away the iniquity of thy servant; for I have done very foolishly.

1 Kings

1Kings 3:9 Give therefore thy servant an understanding heart to judge thy people, that I may discern between good and bad: for who is able to judge this thy so great a people?

1Kings 4:29 And God gave Solomon wisdom and understanding exceeding much, and largeness of heart, even as the sand that is on the sea shore.

1Kings 8:23 And he said, LORD God of Israel, there is no God like thee, in heaven above, or on earth beneath, who keepest covenant and mercy with thy servants that walk before thee with all their heart:

1Kings 8:39 Then hear thou in heaven thy dwelling place, and forgive, and do, and give to every man according to his ways, whose heart thou knowest; (for thou, even thou only, knowest the hearts of all the children of men;)

1Kings 8:61 Let your heart therefore be perfect with the LORD our God, to walk in his statutes, and to keep his commandments, as at this day.

1Kings 10:24 And all the earth sought to Solomon, to hear his wisdom, which God had put in his heart.

1Kings 11:2 Of the nations concerning which the LORD said unto the children of Israel, Ye shall not go in to them, neither shall they come in unto you: for surely they will turn away your heart after their gods: Solomon clave unto these in love.

1Kings 11:4 For it came to pass, when Solomon was old, that his wives turned away his heart after other gods: and his heart was not perfect with the LORD his God, as was the heart of David his father.

1Kings 11:9 And the LORD was angry with Solomon, because his heart was turned from the LORD God of Israel, which had appeared unto him twice,

2 Kings

2Kings 22:19 Because thine heart was tender, and thou hast humbled thyself before the LORD, when thou heardest what I spake against this place, and against the inhabitants thereof, that they should become a desolation and a curse, and hast rent thy clothes, and wept before me; I also have heard thee, saith the LORD.

1 Chronicles

1Chronicles 12:33 Of Zebulun, such as went forth to battle, expert in war, with all instruments of war, fifty thousand, which could keep rank: they were not of double heart.

1Chronicles 17:2 Then Nathan said unto David, Do all that is in thine heart; for God is with thee.

1Chronicles 22:19 Now set your heart and your soul to seek the LORD your God; arise therefore, and build ye the sanctuary of the LORD God, to bring the ark of the covenant of the LORD, and the holy vessels of God, into the house that is to be built to the name of the LORD.

1Chronicles 28:9 And thou, Solomon my son, know thou the God of thy father, and serve him with a perfect heart and with a willing mind: for the LORD searcheth all hearts, and understandeth all the imaginations of the thoughts: if thou seek him, he will be found of thee; but if thou forsake him, he will cast thee off for ever.

1Chronicles 29:9 Then the people rejoiced, for that they offered willingly, because with perfect heart they offered willingly to the LORD: and David the king also rejoiced with great joy.

1Chronicles 29:17 I know also, my God, that thou triest the heart, and hast pleasure in uprightness. As for me, in the uprightness of mine heart I have willingly offered all these things: and now have I seen with joy thy people, which are present here, to offer willingly unto thee.

2 Chronicles

2Chronicles 7:16 For now have I chosen and sanctified this house, that my name may be there for ever: and mine eyes and mine heart shall be there perpetually.

2Chronicles 12:14 And he did evil, because he prepared not his heart to seek the LORD.

2Chronicles 16:9 For the eyes of the LORD run to and fro throughout the whole earth, to shew himself strong in the behalf of them whose heart is perfect toward him. Herein thou hast done foolishly: therefore from henceforth thou shalt have wars.

2Chronicles 25:2 And he did that which was right in the sight of the LORD, but not with a perfect heart.

2Chronicles 29:31 Then Hezekiah answered and said, Now ye have consecrated yourselves unto the LORD, come near and bring sacrifices and thank offerings into the house of the LORD. And the congregation brought in sacrifices and thank offerings; and as many as were of a free heart burnt offerings.

2Chronicles 30:12 Also in Judah the hand of God was to give them one heart to do the commandment of the king and of the princes, by the word of the LORD.

2Chronicles 32:31 Howbeit in the business of the ambassadors of the princes of Babylon, who sent unto him to enquire of the wonder that was done in the land, God left him, to try him, that he might know all that was in his heart.

Ezra

Ezra 7:10 For Ezra had prepared his heart to seek the law of the LORD, and to do it, and to teach in Israel statutes and judgments

Ezra 7:27 Blessed be the LORD God of our fathers, which hath put such a thing as this in the king's heart, to beautify the house of the LORD which is in Jerusalem:

Job

Job 7:17 What is man, that thou shouldest magnify him? and that thou shouldest set thine heart upon him?

Job 41:24 His heart is as firm as a stone; yea, as hard as a piece of the nether millstone.

Psalms

Psalms 7:10 My defence is of God, which saveth the upright in heart.

Psalms 10:3 For the wicked boasteth of his heart's desire, and blesseth the covetous, whom the LORD abhorreth.

Psalms 11:2 For, lo, the wicked bend their bow, they make ready their arrow upon the string, that they may privily shoot at the upright in heart.

Psalms 12:2 They speak vanity every one with his neighbour: with flattering lips and with a double heart do they speak.

Psalms 14:1 To the chief Musician, A Psalm of David. The fool hath said in his heart, There is no God. They are corrupt, they have done abominable works, there is none that doeth good.

Psalms 17:3 Thou hast proved mine heart; thou hast visited me in the night; thou hast tried me, and shalt find nothing; I am purposed that my mouth shall not transgress.

Psalms 19:8 The statutes of the LORD are right, rejoicing the heart: the commandment of the LORD is pure, enlightening the eyes.

Psalms 19:14 Let the words of my mouth, and the meditation of my heart, be acceptable in thy sight, O LORD, my strength, and my redeemer.

Psalms 22:14 I am poured out like water, and all my bones are out of joint: my heart is like wax; it is melted in the midst of my bowels.

Psalms 24:4 He that hath clean hands, and a pure heart; who hath not lifted up his soul unto vanity, nor sworn deceitfully.

Psalms 25:17 The troubles of my heart are enlarged: O bring thou me out of my distresses.

Psalms 26:2 Examine me, O LORD, and prove me; try my reins and my heart.

Psalms 27:3 Though an host should encamp against me, my heart shall not fear: though war should rise against me, in this will I be confident.

Psalms 27:8 When thou saidst, Seek ye my face; my heart said unto thee, Thy face, LORD, will I seek.

Psalms 27:14 Wait on the LORD: be of good courage, and he shall strengthen thine heart: wait, I say, on the LORD.

Psalms 28:7 The LORD is my strength and my shield; my heart trusted in him, and I am helped: therefore my heart greatly rejoiceth; and with my song will I praise him.

Psalms 31:24 Be of good courage, and he shall strengthen your heart, all ye that hope in the LORD.

Psalms 33:11 The counsel of the LORD standeth for ever, the thoughts of his heart to all generations.

Psalms 34:18 The LORD is nigh unto them that are of a broken heart; and saveth such as be of a contrite spirit.

Psalms 36:1 To the chief Musician, A Psalms of David the servant of the LORD. The transgression of the wicked saith within my heart, that there is no fear of God before his eyes.

Psalms 37:4 Delight thyself also in the LORD; and he shall give thee the desires of thine heart.

Psalms 37:31 The law of his God is in his heart; none of his steps shall slide.

Psalms 38:8 I am feeble and sore broken: I have roared by reason of the disquietness of my heart.

Psalms 38:10 My heart panteth, my strength faileth me: as for the light of mine eyes, it also is gone from me.

Psalms 39:3 My heart was hot within me, while I was musing the fire burned: then spake I with my tongue,

Psalms 40:8 I delight to do thy will, O my God: yea, thy law is within my heart.

Psalms 40:12 For innumerable evils have compassed me about: mine iniquities have taken hold upon me, so that I am not able to look up; they are more than the hairs of mine head: therefore my heart faileth me.

Psalms 44:21 Shall not God search this out? for he knoweth the secrets of the heart.

Psalms 45:1 To the chief Musician upon Shoshannim, for the sons of Korah, Maschil, A Song of loves. My heart is inditing a good matter: I speak of the things which I have made touching the king: my tongue is the pen of a ready writer.

Psalms 49:3 My mouth shall speak of wisdom; and the meditation of my heart shall be of understanding.

Psalms 51:10 Create in me a clean heart, O God; and renew a right spirit within me.

Psalms 51:17 The sacrifices of God are a broken spirit: a broken and a contrite heart, O God, thou wilt not despise.

Psalms 53:1 To the chief Musician upon Mahalath, Maschil, A Psalms of David. The fool hath said in his heart, There is no God. Corrupt are they, and have done abominable iniquity: there is none that doeth good.

Psalms 55:21 The words of his mouth were smoother than butter, but war was in his heart: his words were softer than oil, yet were they drawn swords.

Psalms 57:7 My heart is fixed, O God, my heart is fixed: I will sing and give praise.

Psa 61:2 From the end of the earth will I cry unto thee, when my heart is overwhelmed: lead me to the rock that is higher than I.

Psalms 62:8 Trust in him at all times; ye people, pour out your heart before him: God is a refuge for us. Selah.

Psalms 62:10 Trust not in oppression, and become not vain in robbery: if riches increase, set not your heart upon them.

Psalms 64:6 They search out iniquities; they accomplish a diligent search: both the inward thought of every one of them, and the heart, is deep

Psalms 66:18 If I regard iniquity in my heart, the Lord will not hear me:

Psalms 69:20 Reproach hath broken my heart; and I am full of heaviness: and I looked for some to take pity, but there was none; and for comforters, but I found none.

Psalms 69:32 The humble shall see this, and be glad: and your heart shall live that seek God.

Psalms 73:1 A Psalmslm of Asaph. Truly God is good to Israel, even to such as are of a clean heart.

Psalms 73:7 Their eyes stand out with fatness: they have more than heart could wish.

Psalms 73:26 My flesh and my heart faileth: but God is the strength of my heart, and my portion for ever.

Psalms 78:8 And might not be as their fathers, a stubborn and rebellious generation; a generation that set not their heart aright, and whose spirit was not stedfast with God.

Psalms 78:18 And they tempted God in their heart by asking meat for their lust.

Psalms 78:37 For their heart was not right with him, neither were they stedfast in his covenant.

Psalms 78:72 So he fed them according to the integrity of his heart; and guided them by the skilfulness of his hands.

Psalms 84:2 My soul longeth, yea, even fainteth for the courts of the LORD: my heart and my flesh crieth out for the living God.

Psalms 84:5 Blessed is the man whose strength is in thee; in whose heart are the ways of them.

Psalms 86:11 Teach me thy way, O LORD; I will walk in thy truth: unite my heart to fear thy name.

Psalms 86:12 I will praise thee, O Lord my God, with all my heart: and I will glorify thy name for evermore.

Psalms 95:8 Harden not your heart, as in the provocation, and as in the day of temptation in the wilderness:

Psalms 95:10 Forty years long was I grieved with this generation, and said, It is a people that do err in their heart, and they have not known my ways:

Psalms 101:2 I will behave myself wisely in a perfect way. O when wilt thou come unto me? I will walk within my house with a perfect heart.

Psalms 101:4 A froward heart shall depart from me: I will not know a wicked person.

Psalms 101:5 Whoso privily slandereth his neighbour, him will I cut off: him that hath an high look and a proud heart will not I suffer.

Psalms 105:3 Glory ye in his holy name: let the heart of them rejoice that seek the LORD.

Psalms 107:12 Therefore he brought down their heart with labour; they fell down, and there was none to help.

Psalms 108:1 A Song or Psalms of David. O God, my heart is fixed; I will sing and give praise, even with my glory.

Psalms 109:22 For I am poor and needy, and my heart is wounded within me.

Psalms 111:1 Praise ye the LORD. I will praise the LORD with my whole heart, in the assembly of the upright, and in the congregation.

Psalms 112:7 He shall not be afraid of evil tidings: his heart is fixed, trusting in the LORD.

Psalms 112:8 His heart is established, he shall not be afraid, until he see his desire upon his enemies.

Psalms 119:2 Blessed are they that keep his testimonies, and that seek him with the whole heart.

Psalms 119:7 I will praise thee with uprightness of heart, when I shall have learned thy righteous judgments.

Psalms 119:10 With my whole heart have I sought thee: O let me not wander from thy commandments.

Psalms 119:11 Thy word have I hid in mine heart, that I might not sin against thee.

Psalms 119:32 I will run the way of thy commandments, when thou shalt enlarge my heart.

Psalms 119:58 I intreated thy favour with my whole heart: be merciful unto me according to thy word.

Psalms 119:69 The proud have forged a lie against me: but I will keep thy precepts with my whole heart.

Psalms 119:70 Their heart is as fat as grease; but I delight in thy law.

Psalms 119:80 Let my heart be sound in thy statutes; that I be not ashamed.

Psalms 119:161 SCHIN. Princes have persecuted me without a cause: but my heart standeth in awe of thy word.

Psalms 131:1 A Song of degrees of David. LORD, my heart is not haughty, nor mine eyes lofty: neither do I exercise myself in great matters, or in things too high for me.

Psalms 138:1 A Psalm of David. I will praise thee with my whole heart: before the gods will I sing praise unto thee.

Psalms 139:23 Search me, O God, and know my heart: try me, and know my thoughts:

Psalms 140:2 Which imagine mischiefs in their heart; continually are they gathered together for war.

Psalms 143:4 Therefore is my spirit overwhelmed within me; my heart within me is desolate.

Psalms 147:3 He healeth the broken in heart, and bindeth up their wounds.

Proverbs

Proverbs 2:2 So that thou incline thine ear unto wisdom, and apply thine heart to understanding;

Proverbs 2:10 When wisdom entereth into thine heart, and knowledge is pleasant unto thy soul;

Proverbs 3:1 My son, forget not my law; but let thine heart keep my commandments:

Proverbs 3:3 Let not mercy and truth forsake thee: bind them about thy neck; write them upon the table of thine heart:

Proverbs 3:5 Trust in the LORD with all thine heart; and lean not unto thine own understanding.

Proverbs 4:4 He taught me also, and said unto me, Let thine heart retain my words: keep my commandments, and live.

Proverbs 4:21 Let them not depart from thine eyes; keep them in the midst of thine heart.

Proverbs 4:23 Keep thy heart with all diligence; for out of it are the issues of life.

Proverbs 5:12 And say, How have I hated instruction, and my heart despised reproof;

Proverbs 6:14 Frowardness is in his heart, he deviseth mischief continually; he soweth discord.

Proverbs 6:18 An heart that deviseth wicked imaginations, feet that be swift in running to mischief,

Proverbs 6:25 Lust not after her beauty in thine heart; neither let her take thee with her eyelids.

Proverbs 10:8 The wise in heart will receive commandments: but a prating fool shall fall.

Proverbs 10:20 The tongue of the just is as choice silver: the heart of the wicked is little worth.

Proverbs 11:20 They that are of a froward heart are abomination to the LORD: but such as are upright in their way are his delight.

Proverbs 11:29 He that troubleth his own house shall inherit the wind: and the fool shall be servant to the wise of heart.

Proverbs 12:8 A man shall be commended according to his wisdom: but he that is of a perverse heart shall be despised.

Proverbs 12:20 Deceit is in the heart of them that imagine evil: but to the counsellors of peace is joy.

Proverbs 12:23 A prudent man concealeth knowledge: but the heart of fools proclaimeth foolishness.

Proverbs 12:25 Heaviness in the heart of man maketh it stoop: but a good word maketh it glad.

Proverbs 13:12 Hope deferred maketh the heart sick: but when the desire cometh, it is a tree of life.

Proverbs 14:10 The heart knoweth his own bitterness; and a stranger doth not intermeddle with his joy.

Proverbs 14:13 Even in laughter the heart is sorrowful; and the end of that mirth is heaviness.

Proverbs 14:14 The backslider in heart shall be filled with his own ways: and a good man shall be satisfied from himself.

Proverbs 14:30 A sound heart is the life of the flesh: but envy the rottenness of the bones.

Proverbs 14:33 Wisdom resteth in the heart of him that hath understanding: but that which is in the midst of fools is made known.

Proverbs 15:7 The lips of the wise disperse knowledge: but the heart of the foolish doeth not so.

Proverbs 15:13 A merry heart maketh a cheerful countenance: but by sorrow of the heart the spirit is broken.

Proverbs 15:14 The heart of him that hath understanding seeketh knowledge: but the mouth of fools feedeth on foolishness.

Proverbs 15:15 All the days of the afflicted are evil: but he that is of a merry heart hath a continual feast.

Proverbs 15:28 The heart of the righteous studieth to answer: but the mouth of the wicked poureth out evil things.

Proverbs 15:30 The light of the eyes rejoiceth the heart: and a good report maketh the bones fat.

Proverbs 16:1 The preparations of the heart in man, and the answer of the tongue, is from the LORD.

Proverbs 16:5 Every one that is proud in heart is an abomination to the LORD: though hand join in hand, he shall not be unpunished.

Proverbs 16:9 A man's heart deviseth his way: but the LORD directeth his steps.

Proverbs 16:21 The wise in heart shall be called prudent: and the sweetness of the lips increaseth learning.

Proverbs 16:23 The heart of the wise teacheth his mouth, and addeth learning to his lips.

Proverbs 17:16 Wherefore is there a price in the hand of a fool to get wisdom, seeing he hath no heart to it?

Proverbs 17:20 He that hath a froward heart findeth no good: and he that hath a perverse tongue falleth into mischief.

Proverbs 17:22 A merry heart doeth good like a medicine: but a broken spirit drieth the bones.

Proverbs 18:2 A fool hath no delight in understanding, but that his heart may discover itself.

Proverbs 18:12 Before destruction the heart of man is haughty, and before honour is humility.

Proverbs 18:15 The heart of the prudent getteth knowledge; and the ear of the wise seeketh knowledge.

Proverbs 19:3 The foolishness of man perverteth his way: and his heart fretteth against the LORD.

Proverbs 19:21 There are many devices in a man's heart; nevertheless the counsel of the LORD, that shall stand.

Proverbs 20:5 Counsel in the heart of man is like deep water; but a man of understanding will draw it out.

Proverbs 21:1 The king's heart is in the hand of the LORD, as the rivers of water: he turneth it whithersoever he will.

Proverbs 21:4 An high look, and a proud heart, and the plowing of the wicked, is sin.

Proverbs 22:11 He that loveth pureness of heart, for the grace of his lips the king shall be his friend.

Proverbs 22:15 Foolishness is bound in the heart of a child; but the rod of correction shall drive it far from him.

Proverbs 22:17 Bow down thine ear, and hear the words of the wise, and apply thine heart unto my knowledge.

Proverbs 23:7 For as he thinketh in his heart, so is he: Eat and drink, saith he to thee; but his heart is not with thee.

Proverbs 23:17 Let not thine heart envy sinners: but be thou in the fear of the LORD all the day long.

Proverbs 24:2 For their heart studieth destruction, and their lips talk of mischief.

Proverbs 24:12 If thou sayest, Behold, we knew it not; doth not he that pondereth the heart consider it? and he that keepeth thy soul, doth not he know it? and shall not he render to every man according to his works?

Proverbs 24:17 Rejoice not when thine enemy falleth, and let not thine heart be glad when he stumbleth:

Proverbs 25:3 The heaven for height, and the earth for depth, and the heart of kings is unsearchable.

Proverbs 25:20 As he that taketh away a garment in cold weather, and as vinegar upon nitre, so is he that singeth songs to an heavy heart.

Proverbs 26:23 Burning lips and a wicked heart are like a potsherd covered with silver dross.

Proverbs 26:25 When he speaketh fair, believe him not: for there are seven abominations in his heart.

Proverbs 27:9 Ointment and perfume rejoice the heart: so doth the sweetness of a man's friend by hearty counsel.

Proverbs 27:11 My son, be wise, and make my heart glad, that I may answer him that reproacheth me.

Proverbs 27:19 As in water face answereth to face, so the heart of man to man.

Proverbs 28:14 Happy is the man that feareth alway: but he that hardeneth his heart shall fall into mischief.

Proverbs 28:25 He that is of a proud heart stirreth up strife: but he that putteth his trust in the LORD shall be made fat.

Proverbs 28:26 He that trusteth in his own heart is a fool: but whoso walketh wisely, he shall be delivered.

Proverbs 31:11 The heart of her husband doth safely trust in her, so that he shall have no need of spoil.

Ecclesiastes

Ecclesiastes 1:17 And I gave my heart to know wisdom, and to know madness and folly: I perceived that this also is vexation of spirit.

Ecclesiastes 2:1 I said in mine heart, Go to now, I will prove thee with mirth, therefore enjoy pleasure: and, behold, this also is vanity.

Ecclesiastes 2:3 I sought in mine heart to give myself unto wine, yet acquainting mine heart with wisdom; and to lay hold on folly, till I might see what was that good for the sons of men, which they should do under the heaven all the days of their life.

Ecclesiastes 2:10 And whatsoever mine eyes desired I kept not from them, I withheld not my heart from any joy; for my heart rejoiced in all my labour: and this was my portion of all my labour.

Ecclesiastes 2:15 Then said I in my heart, As it happeneth to the fool, so it happeneth even to me; and why was I then more wise? Then I said in my heart, that this also is vanity.

Ecclesiastes 2:20 Therefore I went about to cause my heart to despair of all the labour which I took under the sun.

Ecclesiastes 2:23 For all his days are sorrows, and his travail grief; yea, his heart taketh not rest in the night. This is also vanity.

Ecclesiastes 3:11 He hath made every thing beautiful in his time: also he hath set the world in their heart, so that no man can find out the work that God maketh from the beginning to the end.

Ecclesiastes 3:17 I said in mine heart, God shall judge the righteous and the wicked: for there is a time there for every purpose and for every work.

Ecclesiastes 5:2 Be not rash with thy mouth, and let not thine heart be hasty to utter any thing before God: for God is in heaven, and thou upon earth: therefore let thy words be few.

Ecclesiastes 5:20 For he shall not much remember the days of his life; because God answereth him in the joy of his heart.

Ecclesiastes 7:2 It is better to go to the house of mourning, than to go to the house of feasting: for that is the end of all men; and the living will lay it to his heart.
Ecclesiastes 7:3 Sorrow is better than laughter: for by the sadness of the countenance the heart is made better.
Ecclesiastes 7:4 The heart of the wise is in the house of mourning; but the heart of fools is in the house of mirth.

Ecclesiastes 7:7 Surely oppression maketh a wise man mad; and a gift destroyeth the heart.

Ecclesiastes 7:22 For oftentimes also thine own heart knoweth that thou thyself likewise hast cursed others.

Ecclesiastes 8:5 Whoso keepeth the commandment shall feel no evil thing: and a wise man's heart discerneth both time and judgment.

Ecclesiastes 8:9 All this have I seen, and applied my heart unto every work that is done under the sun: there is a time wherein one man ruleth over another to his own hurt.

Ecclesiastes 8:11 Because sentence against an evil work is not executed speedily, therefore the heart of the sons of men is fully set in them to do evil.

Ecclesiastes 9:3 This is an evil among all things that are done under the sun, that there is one event unto all: yea, also the heart of the sons of men is full of evil, and madness is in their heart while they live, and after that they go to the dead.

Ecclesiastes 10:2 A wise man's heart is at his right hand; but a fool's heart at his left.

Ecclesiastes 11:10 Therefore remove sorrow from thy heart, and put away evil from thy flesh: for childhood and youth are vanity.

Song of Solomon

Song of Solomon 5:2 I sleep, but my heart waketh: it is the voice of my beloved that knocketh, saying, Open to me, my sister, my love, my dove, my undefiled: for my head is filled with dew, and my locks with the drops of the night.

Song of Solomon 8:6 Set me as a seal upon thine heart, as a seal upon thine arm: for love is strong as death; jealousy is cruel as the grave: the coals thereof are coals of fire, which hath a most vehement flame.

Isaiah

Isaiah 6:10 Make the heart of this people fat, and make their ears heavy, and shut their eyes; lest they see with their eyes, and hear with their ears, and understand with their heart, and convert, and be healed.

Isaiah 13:7 Therefore shall all hands be faint, and every man's heart shall melt:

Isaiah 14:13 For thou hast said in thine heart, I will ascend into heaven, I will exalt my throne above the stars of God: I will sit also upon the mount of the congregation, in the sides of the north:

Isaiah 29:13 Wherefore the Lord said, Forasmuch as this people draw near me with their mouth, and with their lips do honour me, but have removed their heart far from me, and their fear toward me is taught by the precept of men:

Isaiah 32:4 The heart also of the rash shall understand knowledge, and the tongue of the stammerers shall be ready to speak plainly.

Isaiah 32:6 For the vile person will speak villany, and his heart will work iniquity, to practise hypocrisy, and to utter error against the LORD, to make empty the soul of the hungry, and he will cause the drink of the thirsty to fail.

Isaiah 33:18 Thine heart shall meditate terror. Where is the scribe? where is the receiver? where is he that counted the towers?

Isaiah 35:4 Say to them that are of a fearful heart, Be strong, fear not: behold, your God will come with vengeance, even God with a recompence; he will come and save you.

Isaiah 42:25 Therefore he hath poured upon him the fury of his anger, and the strength of battle: and it hath set him on fire round about, yet he knew not; and it burned him, yet he laid it not to heart.

Isaiah 44:19 And none considereth in his heart, neither is there knowledge nor understanding to say, I have burned part of it in the fire; yea, also I have baked bread upon the coals thereof; I have roasted flesh, and eaten it: and shall I make the residue thereof an abomination? shall I fall down to the stock of a tree?

Isaiah 44:20 He feedeth on ashes: a deceived heart hath turned him aside, that he cannot deliver his soul, nor say, Is there not a lie in my right hand?

Isaiah 47:8 Therefore hear now this, thou that art given to pleasures, that dwellest carelessly, that sayest in thine heart, I am, and none else beside me; I shall not sit as a widow, neither shall I know the loss of children:

Isaiah 47:10 For thou hast trusted in thy wickedness: thou hast said, None seeth me. Thy wisdom and thy knowledge, it hath perverted thee; and thou hast said in thine heart, I am, and none else beside me.

Isaiah 57:15 For thus saith the high and lofty One that inhabiteth eternity, whose name is Holy; I dwell in the high and holy place, with him also that is of a contrite and humble spirit, to revive the spirit of the humble, and to revive the heart of the contrite ones.

Isaiah 57:17 For the iniquity of his covetousness was I wroth, and smote him: I hid me, and was wroth, and he went on frowardly in the way of his heart.

Isaiah 60:5 Then thou shalt see, and flow together, and thine heart shall fear, and be enlarged; because the abundance of the sea shall be converted unto thee, the forces of the Gentiles shall come unto thee.

Jeremiah

Jeremiah 3:15 And I will give you pastors according to mine heart, which shall feed you with knowledge and understanding.

Jeremiah 3:17 At that time they shall call Jerusalem the throne of the LORD; and all the nations shall be gathered unto it, to the name of the LORD, to Jerusalem: neither shall they walk any more after the imagination of their evil heart.

Jeremiah 4:4 Circumcise yourselves to the LORD, and take away the foreskins of your heart, ye men of Judah and inhabitants of Jerusalem: lest my fury come forth like fire, and burn that none can quench it, because of the evil of your doings.

Jeremiah 4:14 O Jerusalem, wash thine heart from wickedness, that thou mayest be saved. How long shall thy vain thoughts lodge within thee?

Jeremiah 4:18 Thy way and thy doings have procured these things unto thee; this is thy wickedness, because it is bitter, because it reacheth unto thine heart.

Jeremiah 5:23 But this people hath a revolting and a rebellious heart; they are revolted and gone.

Jeremiah 7:24 But they hearkened not, nor inclined their ear, but walked in the counsels and in the imagination of their evil heart, and went backward, and not forward.

Jeremiah 8:18 When I would comfort myself against sorrow, my heart is faint in me.

Jeremiah 9:8 Their tongue is as an arrow shot out; it speaketh deceit: one speaketh peaceably to his neighbour with his mouth, but in heart he layeth his wait.

Jeremiah 9:14 But have walked after the imagination of their own heart, and after Baalim, which their fathers taught them:

Jeremiah 11:20 But, O LORD of hosts, that judgest righteously, that triest the reins and the heart, let me see thy vengeance on them: for unto thee have I revealed my cause.

Jeremiah 12:3 But thou, O LORD, knowest me: thou hast seen me, and tried mine heart toward thee: pull them out like sheep for the slaughter, and prepare them for the day of slaughter.

Jeremiah 12:11 They have made it desolate, and being desolate it mourneth unto me; the whole land is made desolate, because no man layeth it to heart.

Jeremiah 13:10 This evil people, which refuse to hear my words, which walk in the imagination of their heart, and walk after other gods, to serve them, and to worship them, shall even be as this girdle, which is good for nothing.

Jeremiah 13:22 And if thou say in thine heart, Wherefore come these things upon me? For the greatness of thine iniquity are thy skirts discovered, and thy heels made bare.

Jeremiah 14:14 Then the LORD said unto me, The prophets prophesy lies in my name: I sent them not, neither have I commanded them, neither spake unto them: they prophesy unto you a false vision and divination, and a thing of nought, and the deceit of their heart.

Jeremiah 15:16 Thy words were found, and I did eat them; and thy word was unto me the joy and rejoicing of mine heart: for I am called by thy name, O LORD God of hosts.

Jeremiah 17:5 Thus saith the LORD; Cursed be the man that trusteth in man, and maketh flesh his arm, and whose heart departeth from the LORD.

Jeremiah 17:9 The heart is deceitful above all things, and desperately wicked: who can know it?

Jeremiah 17:10 I the LORD search the heart, I try the reins, even to give every man according to his ways, and according to the fruit of his doings.

Jeremiah 18:12 And they said, There is no hope: but we will walk after our own devices, and we will every one do the imagination of his evil heart.

Jeremiah 20:9 Then I said, I will not make mention of him, nor speak any more in his name. But his word was in mine heart as a burning fire shut up in my bones, and I was weary with forbearing, and I could not stay.

Jeremiah 23:16 Thus saith the LORD of hosts, Hearken not unto the words of the prophets that prophesy unto you: they make you vain: they speak a vision of their own heart, and not out of the mouth of the LORD.
Jeremiah 23:17 They say still unto them that despise me, The LORD hath said, Ye shall have peace; and they say unto every one that walketh after the imagination of his own heart, No evil shall come upon you.

Jeremiah 23:20 The anger of the LORD shall not return, until he have executed, and till he have performed the thoughts of his heart: in the latter days ye shall consider it perfectly.

Jeremiah 23:26 How long shall this be in the heart of the prophets that prophesy lies? yea, they are prophets of the deceit of their own heart;

Jeremiah 24:7 And I will give them an heart to know me, that I am the LORD: and they shall be my people, and I will be their God: for they shall return unto me with their whole heart.

Jeremiah 29:13 And ye shall seek me, and find me, when ye shall search for me with all your heart.

Jeremiah 30:21 And their nobles shall be of themselves, and their governor shall proceed from the midst of them;

and I will cause him to draw near, and he shall approach unto me: for who is this that engaged his heart to approach unto me? saith the LORD.

Jeremiah 32:39 And I will give them one heart, and one way, that they may fear me for ever, for the good of them, and of their children after them:

Jeremiah 32:41 Yea, I will rejoice over them to do them good, and I will plant them in this land assuredly with my whole heart and with my whole soul.

Jeremiah 48:29 We have heard the pride of Moab, (he is exceeding proud) his loftiness, and his arrogancy, and his pride, and the haughtiness of his heart.

Jeremiah 51:46 And lest your heart faint, and ye fear for the rumour that shall be heard in the land; a rumour shall both come one year, and after that in another year shall come a rumour, and violence in the land, ruler against ruler.

Lamentations

Lamentations 1:20 Behold, O LORD; for I am in distress: my bowels are troubled; mine heart is turned within me; for I have grievously rebelled: abroad the sword bereaveth, at home there is as death.

Lamentations 1:22 Let all their wickedness come before thee; and do unto them, as thou hast done unto me for all my transgressions: for my sighs are many, and my heart is faint.

Lamentations 2:19 Arise, cry out in the night: in the beginning of the watches pour out thine heart like water before the face of the Lord: lift up thy hands toward him for the life of thy young children, that faint for hunger in the top of every street.

Lamentations 3:41 Let us lift up our heart with our hands unto God in the heavens.

Lamentations 3:51 Mine eye affecteth mine heart because of all the daughters of my city.

Lamentations 3:65 Give them sorrow of heart, thy curse unto them.

Lamentations 5:15 The joy of our heart is ceased; our dance is turned into mourning.

Lamentations 5:17 For this our heart is faint; for these things our eyes are dim.

Ezekiel

Ezekiel 6:9 And they that escape of you shall remember me among the nations whither they shall be carried captives, because I am broken with their whorish heart, which hath departed from me, and with their eyes, which go a whoring after their idols: and they shall lothe themselves for the evils which they have committed in all their abominations.

Ezekiel 11:19 And I will give them one heart, and I will put a new spirit within you; and I will take the stony heart out of their flesh, and will give them an heart of flesh: Ezekiel 11:21 But as for them whose heart walketh after the heart of their detestable things and their abominations, I will recompense their way upon their own heads, saith the Lord GOD.

Ezekiel 13:17 Likewise, thou son of man, set thy face against the daughters of thy people, which prophesy out of their own heart; and prophesy thou against them,

Ezekiel 13:22 Because with lies ye have made the heart of the righteous sad, whom I have not made sad; and strengthened the hands of the wicked, that he should not return from his wicked way, by promising him life:

Ezekiel 14:3 Son of man, these men have set up their idols in their heart, and put the stumblingblock of their iniquity before their face: should I be enquired of at all by them?

Ezekiel 14:4 Therefore speak unto them, and say unto them, Thus saith the Lord GOD; Every man of the house of Israel that setteth up his idols in his heart, and putteth the stumblingblock of his iniquity before his face, and cometh to the prophet; I the LORD will answer him that cometh according to the multitude of his idols;

Ezekiel 14:5 That I may take the house of Israel in their own heart, because they are all estranged from me through their idols.

Ezekiel 14:7 For every one of the house of Israel, or of the stranger that sojourneth in Israel, which separateth himself from me, and setteth up his idols in his heart, and putteth the stumblingblock of his iniquity before his face, and cometh to a prophet to enquire of him concerning me; I the LORD will answer him by myself:

Ezekiel 16:30 How weak is thine heart, saith the Lord GOD, seeing thou doest all these things, the work of an imperious whorish woman;

Ezekiel 18:31 Cast away from you all your transgressions, whereby ye have transgressed; and make you a new heart and a new spirit: for why will ye die, O house of Israel?

Ezekiel 20:16 Because they despised my judgments, and walked not in my statutes, but polluted my sabbaths: for their heart went after their idols.

Ezekiel 21:7 And it shall be, when they say unto thee, Wherefore sighest thou? that thou shalt answer, For the tidings; because it cometh: and every heart shall melt, and all hands shall be feeble, and every spirit shall faint, and all knees shall be weak as water: behold, it cometh, and shall be brought to pass, saith the Lord GOD.

Ezekiel 21:15 I have set the point of the sword against all their gates, that their heart may faint, and their ruins be multiplied: ah! it is made bright, it is wrapped up for the slaughter.

Ezekiel 22:14 Can thine heart endure, or can thine hands be strong, in the days that I shall deal with thee? I the LORD have spoken it, and will do it.

Ezekiel 25:6 For thus saith the Lord GOD; Because thou hast clapped thine hands, and stamped with the feet, and rejoiced in heart with all thy despite against the land of Israel;

Ezekiel 25:15 Thus saith the Lord GOD; Because the Philistines have dealt by revenge, and have taken vengeance with a despiteful heart, to destroy it for the old hatred;

Ezekiel 28:2 Son of man, say unto the prince of Tyrus, Thus saith the Lord GOD; Because thine heart is lifted up, and thou hast said, I am a God, I sit in the seat of God, in the midst of the seas; yet thou art a man, and not God, though thou set thine heart as the heart of God:

Ezekiel 28:5 By thy great wisdom and by thy traffick hast thou increased thy riches, and thine heart is lifted up because of thy riches:

Ezekiel 28:6 Therefore thus saith the Lord GOD; Because thou hast set thine heart as the heart of God;

Ezekiel 28:17 Thine heart was lifted up because of thy beauty, thou hast corrupted thy wisdom by reason of thy brightness: I will cast thee to the ground, I will lay thee before kings, that they may behold thee.

Ezekiel 33:31 And they come unto thee as the people cometh, and they sit before thee as my people, and they hear thy words, but they will not do them: for with their mouth they shew much love, but their heart goeth after their covetousness.

Ezekiel 36:26 A new heart also will I give you, and a new spirit will I put within you: and I will take away the stony heart out of your flesh, and I will give you an heart of flesh.

Ezekiel 40:4 And the man said unto me, Son of man, behold with thine eyes, and hear with thine ears, and set thine heart upon all that I shall shew thee; for to the intent that I might shew them unto thee art thou brought hither: declare all that thou seest to the house of Israel.

Ezekiel 44:7 In that ye have brought into my sanctuary strangers, uncircumcised in heart, and uncircumcised in flesh, to be in my sanctuary, to pollute it, even my house, when ye offer my bread, the fat and the blood, and they have broken my covenant because of all your abominations.

Ezekiel 44:9 Thus saith the Lord GOD; No stranger, uncircumcised in heart, nor uncircumcised in flesh, shall enter into my sanctuary, of any stranger that is among the children of Israel.

Daniel

Daniel 1:8 But Daniel purposed in his heart that he would not defile himself with the portion of the king's meat, nor with the wine which he drank: therefore he requested of the prince of the eunuchs that he might not defile himself.

Daniel 4:16 Let his heart be changed from man's, and let a beast's heart be given unto him; and let seven times pass over him.

Daniel 5:20 But when his heart was lifted up, and his mind hardened in pride, he was deposed from his kingly throne, and they took his glory from him:

Daniel 5:21 And he was driven from the sons of men; and his heart was made like the beasts, and his dwelling was with the wild asses: they fed him with grass like oxen, and his body was wet with the dew of heaven; till he knew that the most high God ruled in the kingdom of men, and that he appointeth over it whomsoever he will.

Daniel 5:22 And thou his son, O Belshazzar, hast not humbled thine heart, though thou knewest all this;

Daniel 6:14 Then the king, when he heard these words, was sore displeased with himself, and set his heart on Daniel to deliver him: and he laboured till the going down of the sun to deliver him.

Daniel 7:28 Hitherto is the end of the matter. As for me Daniel, my cogitations much troubled me, and my countenance changed in me: but I kept the matter in my heart.

Daniel 10:12 Then said he unto me, Fear not, Daniel: for from the first day that thou didst set thine heart to understand, and to chasten thyself before thy God, thy words were heard, and I am come for thy words.

Hosea

Hosea 4:11 Whoredom and wine and new wine take away the heart.

Hosea 7:6 For they have made ready their heart like an oven, whiles they lie in wait: their baker sleepeth all the night; in the morning it burneth as a flaming fire.

Hosea 7:11 Ephraim also is like a silly dove without heart: they call to Egypt, they go to Assyria.

Hosea 7:14 And they have not cried unto me with their heart, when they howled upon their beds: they assemble themselves for corn and wine, and they rebel against me.

Hosea 10:2 Their heart is divided; now shall they be found faulty: he shall break down their altars, he shall spoil their images.

Hosea 13:6 According to their pasture, so were they filled; they were filled, and their heart was exalted; therefore have they forgotten me.

Joel

Joel 2:12 Therefore also now, saith the LORD, turn ye even to me with all your heart, and with fasting, and with weeping, and with mourning:
Joel 2:13 And rend your heart, and not your garments, and turn unto the LORD your God: for he is gracious and merciful, slow to anger, and of great kindness, and repenteth him of the evil.

Obadiah

Obadiah 1:3 The pride of thine heart hath deceived thee, thou that dwellest in the clefts of the rock, whose habitation is high; that saith in his heart, Who shall bring me down to the ground?

Zephaniah

Zephaniah 1:12 And it shall come to pass at that time, that I will search Jerusalem with candles, and punish the men that are settled on their lees: that say in their heart, The LORD will not do good, neither will he do evil.

Zephaniah 2:15 This is the rejoicing city that dwelt carelessly, that said in her heart, I am, and there is none beside me: how is she become a desolation, a place for beasts to lie down in! every one that passeth by her shall hiss, and wag his hand.

Zechariah

Zechariah 7:10 And oppress not the widow, nor the fatherless, the stranger, nor the poor; and let none of you imagine evil against his brother in your heart.

Malachi

Malachi 2:2 If ye will not hear, and if ye will not lay it to heart, to give glory unto my name, saith the LORD of hosts, I will even send a curse upon you, and I will curse your blessings: yea, I have cursed them already, because ye do not lay it to heart.

Malachi 4:6 And he shall turn the heart of the fathers to the children, and the heart of the children to their fathers, lest I come and smite the earth with a curse.

NEW TESTAMENT

Matthew

Matthew 5:8 Blessed are the pure in heart: for they shall see God.

Matthew 5:28 But I say unto you, That whosoever looketh on a woman to lust after her hath committed adultery with her already in his heart.

Matthew 6:21 For where your treasure is, there will your heart be also.

Matthew 11:29 Take my yoke upon you, and learn of me; for I am meek and lowly in heart: and ye shall find rest unto your souls.

Matthew 12:34 O generation of vipers, how can ye, being evil, speak good things? for out of the abundance of the heart the mouth speaketh.

Matthew 12:35 A good man out of the good treasure of the heart bringeth forth good things: and an evil man out of the evil treasure bringeth forth evil things.

Matthew 13:15 For this people's heart is waxed gross, and their ears are dull of hearing, and their eyes they have closed; lest at any time they should see with their eyes, and hear with their ears, and should understand with their heart, and should be converted, and I should heal them.

Matthew 13:19 When any one heareth the word of the kingdom, and understandeth it not, then cometh the wicked one, and catcheth away that which was sown in his heart. This is he which received seed by the way side.

Matthew 15:8 This people draweth nigh unto me with their mouth, and honoureth me with their lips; but their heart is far from me.

Matthew 15:18 But those things which proceed out of the mouth come forth from the heart; and they defile the man.
Matthew 15:19 For out of the heart proceed evil thoughts, murders, adulteries, fornications, thefts, false witness, blasphemies:

Matthew 22:37 Jesus said unto him, Thou shalt love the Lord thy God with all thy heart, and with all thy soul, and with all thy mind.

Mark

Mark 6:52 For they considered not the miracle of the loaves: for their heart was hardened.

Mark 7:6 He answered and said unto them, Well hath Esaias prophesied of you hypocrites, as it is written, This people honoureth me with their lips, but their heart is far from me.

Mark 7:19 Because it entereth not into his heart, but into the belly, and goeth out into the draught, purging all meats?

Mark 7:21 For from within, out of the heart of men, proceed evil thoughts, adulteries, fornications, murders,

Mark 8:17 And when Jesus knew it, he saith unto them, Why reason ye, because ye have no bread? perceive ye not yet, neither understand? have ye your heart yet hardened?

Mark 10:5 And Jesus answered and said unto them, For the hardness of your heart he wrote you this precept.

Mark 11:23 For verily I say unto you, That whosoever shall say unto this mountain, Be thou removed, and be thou cast into the sea; and shall not doubt in his heart, but shall believe that those things which he saith shall come to pass; he shall have whatsoever he saith.

Mark 12:30 And thou shalt love the Lord thy God with all thy heart, and with all thy soul, and with all thy mind, and with all thy strength: this is the first commandment.

Mark 12:33 And to love him with all the heart, and with all the understanding, and with all the soul, and with all the strength, and to love his neighbour as himself, is more than all whole burnt offerings and sacrifices.

Mark 16:14 Afterward he appeared unto the eleven as they sat at meat, and upbraided them with their unbelief and hardness of heart, because they believed not them which had seen him after he was risen.

Luke

Luke 2:19 But Mary kept all these things, and pondered them in her heart.

Luke 2:51 And he went down with them, and came to Nazareth, and was subject unto them: but his mother kept all these sayings in her heart.

Luke 6:45 A good man out of the good treasure of his heart bringeth forth that which is good; and an evil man out of the evil treasure of his heart bringeth forth that which is evil: for of the abundance of the heart his mouth speaketh.

Luke 8:15 But that on the good ground are they, which in an honest and good heart, having heard the word, keep it, and bring forth fruit with patience.

Luke 9:47 And Jesus, perceiving the thought of their heart, took a child, and set him by him,

Luke 10:27 And he answering said, Thou shalt love the Lord thy God with all thy heart, and with all thy soul, and with all thy strength, and with all thy mind; and thy neighbour as thyself.

Luke 12:34 For where your treasure is, there will your heart be also.

Luke 12:45 But and if that servant say in his heart, My lord delayeth his coming; and shall begin to beat the menservants and maidens, and to eat and drink, and to be drunken;

Luke 24:25 Then he said unto them, O fools, and slow of heart to believe all that the prophets have spoken:

Luke 24:32 And they said one to another, Did not our heart burn within us, while he talked with us by the way, and while he opened to us the scriptures?

John

John 12:40 He hath blinded their eyes, and hardened their heart; that they should not see with their eyes, nor understand with their heart, and be converted, and I should heal them.

John 13:2 And supper being ended, the devil having now put into the heart of Judas Iscariot, Simon's son, to betray him;

John 14:1 Let not your heart be troubled: ye believe in God, believe also in me.

John 14:27 Peace I leave with you, my peace I give unto you: not as the world giveth, give I unto you. Let not your heart be troubled, neither let it be afraid.

John 16:6 But because I have said these things unto you, sorrow hath filled your heart.

John 16:22 And ye now therefore have sorrow: but I will see you again, and your heart shall rejoice, and your joy no man taketh from you.

Acts

Acts 2:37 Now when they heard this, they were pricked in their heart, and said unto Peter and to the rest of the apostles, Men and brethren, what shall we do?

Acts 2:46 And they, continuing daily with one accord in the temple, and breaking bread from house to house, did eat their meat with gladness and singleness of heart,

Acts 4:32 And the multitude of them that believed were of one heart and of one soul: neither said any of them that ought of the things which he possessed was his own; but they had all things common.

Acts 5:3 But Peter said, Ananias, why hath Satan filled thine heart to lie to the Holy Ghost, and to keep back part of the price of the land?

Acts 5:4 Whiles it remained, was it not thine own? and after it was sold, was it not in thine own power? why hast thou conceived this thing in thine heart? thou hast not lied unto men, but unto God.

Acts 5:33 When they heard that, they were cut to the heart, and took counsel to slay them.

Acts 7:23 And when he was full forty years old, it came into his heart to visit his brethren the children of Israel.

Acts 7:51 Ye stiffnecked and uncircumcised in heart and ears, ye do always resist the Holy Ghost: as your fathers did, so do ye.

Acts 7:54 When they heard these things, they were cut to the heart, and they gnashed on him with their teeth.

Acts 8:21 Thou hast neither part nor lot in this matter: for thy heart is not right in the sight of God.

Acts 8:22 Repent therefore of this thy wickedness, and pray God, if perhaps the thought of thine heart may be forgiven thee.

Acts 8:37 And Philip said, If thou believest with all thine heart, thou mayest. And he answered and said, I believe that Jesus Christ is the Son of God.

Acts 13:22 And when he had removed him, he raised up unto them David to be their king; to whom also he gave testimony, and said, I have found David the son of Jesse, a man after mine own heart, which shall fulfil all my will.

Acts 16:14 And a certain woman named Lydia, a seller of purple, of the city of Thyatira, which worshipped God, heard us: whose heart the Lord opened, that she attended unto the things which were spoken of Paul.

Acts 28:27 For the heart of this people is waxed gross, and their ears are dull of hearing, and their eyes have they closed; lest they should see with their eyes, and hear with their ears, and understand with their heart, and should be converted, and I should heal them.

Romans

Romans 1:21 Because that, when they knew God, they glorified him not as God, neither were thankful; but became vain in their imaginations, and their foolish heart was darkened.

Romans 2:5 But after thy hardness and impenitent heart treasurest up unto thyself wrath against the day of wrath and revelation of the righteous judgment of God;

Romans 2:29 But he is a Jew, which is one inwardly; and circumcision is that of the heart, in the spirit, and not in the letter; whose praise is not of men, but of God.

Romans 6:17 But God be thanked, that ye were the servants of sin, but ye have obeyed from the heart that form of doctrine which was delivered you.

Romans 10:8 But what saith it? The word is nigh thee, even in thy mouth, and in thy heart: that is, the word of faith, which we preach;

Romans 10:9 That if thou shalt confess with thy mouth the Lord Jesus, and shalt believe in thine heart that God hath raised him from the dead, thou shalt be saved.

Romans 10:10 For with the heart man believeth unto righteousness; and with the mouth confession is made unto salvation.

1 Corinthians

1 Corinthians 2:9 But as it is written, Eye hath not seen, nor ear heard, neither have entered into the heart of man, the things which God hath prepared for them that love him.

1 Corinthians 7:37 Nevertheless he that standeth stedfast in his heart, having no necessity, but hath power over his own will, and hath so decreed in his heart that he will keep his virgin, doeth well.

1 Corinthians 14:25 And thus are the secrets of his heart made manifest; and so falling down on his face he will worship God, and report that God is in you of a truth.

2 Corinthians

2Corinthians 2:4 For out of much affliction and anguish of heart I wrote unto you with many tears; not that ye should be grieved, but that ye might know the love which I have more abundantly unto you.

2Corinthians 3:3 Forasmuch as ye are manifestly declared to be the epistle of Christ ministered by us, written not with ink, but with the Spirit of the living God; not in tables of stone, but in fleshy tables of the heart.

2Corinthians 6:11 O ye Corinthians, our mouth is open unto you, our heart is enlarged.

2Corinthians 9:7 Every man according as he purposeth in his heart, so let him give; not grudgingly, or of necessity: for God loveth a cheerful giver.

Ephesians

Ephesians 4:18 Having the understanding darkened, being alienated from the life of God through the ignorance that is in them, because of the blindness of their heart:

Ephesians 5:19 Speaking to yourselves in psalms and hymns and spiritual songs, singing and making melody in your heart to the Lord;

Ephesians 6:5 Servants, be obedient to them that are your masters according to the flesh, with fear and trembling, in singleness of your heart, as unto Christ;

Ephesians 6:6 Not with eyeservice, as menpleasers; but as the servants of Christ, doing the will of God from the heart;

Colossians

Colossians 3:22 Servants, obey in all things your masters according to the flesh; not with eyeservice, as menpleasers; but in singleness of heart, fearing God:

1 Timothy

1Timothy 1:5 Now the end of the commandment is charity out of a pure heart, and of a good conscience, and of faith unfeigned:

2 Timothy

2Timothy 2:22 Flee also youthful lusts: but follow righteousness, faith, charity, peace, with them that call on the Lord out of a pure heart.

Hebrews

Hebrews 3:10 Wherefore I was grieved with that generation, and said, They do alway err in their heart; and they have not known my ways.

Hebrews 3:12 Take heed, brethren, lest there be in any of you an evil heart of unbelief, in departing from the living God.

Hebrews 4:12 For the word of God is quick, and powerful, and sharper than any two-edged sword, piercing even to the dividing asunder of soul and spirit, and of the joints and marrow, and is a discerner of the thoughts and intents of the heart.

Hebrews 10:22 Let us draw near with a true heart in full assurance of faith, having our hearts sprinkled from an evil conscience, and our bodies washed with pure water.

Hebrews 13:9 Be not carried about with divers and strange doctrines. For it is a good thing that the heart be established with grace; not with meats, which have not profited them that have been occupied therein.

James

James 1:26 If any man among you seem to be religious, and bridleth not his tongue, but deceiveth his own heart, this man's religion is vain.

1 Peter

1Peter 1:22 Seeing ye have purified your souls in obeying the truth through the Spirit unto unfeigned love of the brethren, see that ye love one another with a pure heart fervently:

1Peter 3:4 But let it be the hidden man of the heart, in that which is not corruptible, even the ornament of a meek and quiet spirit, which is in the sight of God of great price.

2Peter

2Peter 2:14 Having eyes full of adultery, and that cannot cease from sin; beguiling unstable souls: an heart they have exercised with covetous practices; cursed children:

1 John

1John 3:20 For if our heart condemn us, God is greater than our heart, and knoweth all things.

1John 3:21 Beloved, if our heart condemn us not, then have we confidence toward God.